Kids' Cake Mix FUN
and more

pil

Publications International, Ltd.
Favorite Brand Name Recipes at www.fbnr.com

Recipe Development: Bev Bennett, Alison Reich and Marcia Kay Stanley

Photography on pages 7, 9, 15, 19, 21, 23, 29, 35, 39, 41, 53, 55, 61, 65, 67, 69, 71, 91, 95, 101, 103, 115, 117, 119 and 135 by Proffitt Photography, Ltd., Chicago.

Photography on pages 11, 17, 25, 27, 33, 45, 47, 49, 51, 57, 73, 79, 93, 97, 105, 113, 123, 129, 131 and 133 by Chris Cassidy Photography, Inc.

Pictured on the front cover *(clockwise from top left):* Marshmallow Fudge Sundae Cupcakes *(page 68),* Ice Cream Sandwiches *(page 48),* Miss Pinky the Pig Cupcakes *(page 70)* and Cranberry Gems *(page 26).*

Pictured on the back cover: Sleepover Cake *(page 128).*

ISBN-13: 978-1-4127-2221-6
ISBN-10: 1-4127-2221-7

Library of Congress Control Number: 2005920750

Manufactured in China.

8 7 6 5 4 3 2 1

Microwave Cooking: Microwave ovens vary in wattage. Use the cooking times as guidelines and check for doneness before adding more time.

Contents

Cake Mix Basics

So many occasions, so little time!

Whether you need cookies for a classroom snack, cupcakes for a bake sale or an unforgettable birthday cake, you might not have time for traditional, made-from-scratch baking. But you don't need complicated recipes with lots of ingredients to create beautiful, crowd-pleasing treats. Baking should be easy—and fun!

Cake Mix Fun puts the fun back in baking, with simple recipes and easy-to-follow instructions. Combining cake mix with a few additional ingredients is the best way to create wonderful desserts with minimal time and effort. And unlike scratch baking, where a little mistake might throw off a whole recipe, cake mixes are actually formulated to withstand inconsistencies such as overmixing and pan size discrepancies. So even if you're a baking novice, you're almost guaranteed to succeed.

Cake Mix Confusion

While baking with cake mixes is easy, there are still a few important things to know before you begin. All cake mixes are not the same. Make sure you read the recipe carefully to see what kind of cake mix is required, then look closely at your options in the supermarket and check the following:

Package size

Most cake mixes are for two-layer cakes (about 18 ounces) but some are for one-layer cakes (about 9 ounces). The recipe will specify which size to use.

Pudding or no pudding

The majority of the cake mixes available today contain pudding, which is always stated on the package—if the box does not say the mix contains pudding then there is no pudding in the mix. Many of the recipes in this book specify which type of mix to use; if no specific type is given, you can use whichever kind you prefer. (Keep in mind that mixes with pudding should never be used when a recipe contains instant pudding as an ingredient.)

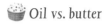 Oil vs. butter

The directions on cake mix packages list the ingredients you need to add to the mix, usually water, eggs and vegetable oil. Only a few mixes call for butter instead of oil, and these mixes will have the words "butter recipe" somewhere on the package. Using butter results in a slightly different flavor and texture in the final product. Just a few recipes in this book require a butter recipe mix; otherwise you should use the standard mixes that call for oil and are far more prevalent on the supermarket shelves.

Cake Mix Fundamentals

Follow these simple guidelines for successful baking:

• Read the entire recipe before beginning to make sure you have all the necessary ingredients and baking utensils.

• Remove butter and cream cheese from the refrigerator to soften, if necessary.

• Adjust the oven racks and preheat the oven. Check the oven temperature for accuracy with an oven thermometer.

• Use standardized measuring spoons and cups when measuring dry ingredients. Fill the appropriate measuring spoon or cup to overflowing and level it off with a metal spatula or the flat edge of a knife.

• Use a standard glass or plastic measuring cup with calibrations marked on the side when measuring liquid ingredients. Place the cup on a flat surface, fill to the desired mark and check the measurement at eye level.

• Always use the pan size specified in the recipe, and prepare the pan as directed in the recipe or the package directions.

• When substituting glass bakeware in recipes that call for baking pans, reduce the oven temperature by 25°F.

• Follow the recipe directions and baking times. Check for doneness using the test given in the recipe.

Lip-Smackin' Snack Cakes

S'MORE SNACK CAKE

Makes 24 servings

1 package (18¼ ounces) yellow cake mix with pudding in the mix, plus ingredients to prepare mix

1 cup chocolate chunks, divided

1½ cups miniature marshmallows

1 cup bear-shaped graham crackers (honey or chocolate flavor)

1. Preheat oven to 350°F. Grease 13×9-inch baking pan.

2. Prepare cake mix according to package directions. Spread batter in prepared pan. Sprinkle with ½ cup chocolate chunks.

3. Bake 30 minutes. Remove cake from oven; sprinkle with remaining ½ cup chocolate chunks and marshmallows. Arrange bear-shaped graham crackers evenly over top of cake as shown in photo.

4. Return cake to oven; bake 8 minutes or until marshmallows are golden brown. Cool completely before cutting.

S'More Snack Cake

TOPSY-TURVY BANANA CRUNCH CAKE

Makes 9 servings

1/3 cup uncooked old-fashioned oats
3 tablespoons packed brown sugar
1 tablespoon all-purpose flour
1/4 teaspoon ground cinnamon
2 tablespoons butter
2 tablespoons chopped pecans
1 package (9 ounces) yellow cake mix *without* pudding in the mix
1/2 cup sour cream
1/2 cup mashed banana (about 1 medium)
1 egg

1. Preheat oven to 350°F. Lightly grease 8-inch square baking pan.

2. Combine oats, brown sugar, flour and cinnamon in small bowl. Cut in butter with pastry blender or 2 knives until mixture is crumbly. Stir in pecans.

3. Beat cake mix, sour cream, banana and egg in medium bowl with electric mixer at low speed about 1 minute or until blended. Increase speed to medium; beat 1 to 2 minutes or until smooth. Spoon half of batter into prepared pan; sprinkle with half of oat topping. Repeat with remaining batter and topping.

4. Bake 25 to 30 minutes or until toothpick inserted into center comes out clean. Cool completely on wire rack.

TOPSY-TURVY BANANA CRUNCH CAKE

Makes 9 servings

⅓ cup uncooked old-fashioned oats
3 tablespoons packed brown sugar
1 tablespoon all-purpose flour
¼ teaspoon ground cinnamon
2 tablespoons butter
2 tablespoons chopped pecans
1 package (9 ounces) yellow cake mix *without* pudding in the mix
½ cup sour cream
½ cup mashed banana (about 1 medium)
1 egg

1. Preheat oven to 350°F. Lightly grease 8-inch square baking pan.

2. Combine oats, brown sugar, flour and cinnamon in small bowl. Cut in butter with pastry blender or 2 knives until mixture is crumbly. Stir in pecans.

3. Beat cake mix, sour cream, banana and egg in medium bowl with electric mixer at low speed about 1 minute or until blended. Increase speed to medium; beat 1 to 2 minutes or until smooth. Spoon half of batter into prepared pan; sprinkle with half of oat topping. Repeat with remaining batter and topping.

4. Bake 25 to 30 minutes or until toothpick inserted into center comes out clean. Cool completely on wire rack.

DOUBLE CHOCOLATE CHIP SNACK CAKE

Makes 8 to 10 servings

1 package (18¼ ounces) devil's food cake mix with pudding in the mix, divided
2 eggs
½ cup water
¼ cup vegetable oil
½ teaspoon cinnamon
1 cup semisweet chocolate chips, divided
¼ cup packed brown sugar
2 tablespoons butter or margarine, melted
¾ cup white chocolate chips

1. Preheat oven to 350°F. Grease 9-inch round cake pan. Reserve ¾ cup cake mix; set aside.

2. Pour remaining cake mix into large bowl. Add eggs, water, oil and cinnamon; beat with electric mixer at medium speed 2 minutes. Remove ½ cup batter.* Spread remaining batter in prepared pan; sprinkle with ½ cup chocolate chips.

3. Combine reserved cake mix and brown sugar in medium bowl. Stir in butter and remaining ½ cup chocolate chips; mix well. Sprinkle mixture over batter in pan.

4. Bake 35 to 40 minutes or until toothpick inserted into center comes out clean and cake springs back when lightly touched.

5. Place white chocolate chips in resealable plastic food storage bag; seal bag. Microwave at HIGH 10 seconds; knead bag gently. Repeat until chips are melted. Cut off ¼ inch from corner of bag with scissors; drizzle chocolate over cake. Cool cake on wire rack before cutting into wedges.

If desired, extra batter can be used for cupcakes: Pour batter into two foil or paper cupcake liners placed on baking sheet; bake at 350°F 20 to 25 minutes or until toothpick inserted into centers comes out clean.

BLUEBERRY CREAM CHEESE POUND CAKE

Makes 1 (9-inch) pound cake

1 package (16 ounces) pound cake mix, divided
1½ cups fresh blueberries
5 ounces cream cheese, softened
2 eggs
¾ cup milk
Powdered sugar (optional)

1. Preheat oven to 350°F. Grease 9×5-inch loaf pan.

2. Place ¼ cup cake mix in medium bowl; add blueberries and toss until well coated.

3. Beat cream cheese in large bowl with electric mixer at medium speed 1 minute or until light and fluffy. Add eggs, one at a time, beating well after each addition.

4. Add remaining cake mix alternately with milk, beginning and ending with cake mix, beating well after each addition. Beat 1 minute at medium speed or until light and fluffy.

5. Fold blueberry mixture into batter; pour batter into prepared pan. Bake 55 to 60 minutes or until toothpick inserted into center comes out clean.

6. Cool in pan on wire rack 10 minutes. Remove cake from pan; cool completely on wire rack. Sprinkle with powdered sugar, if desired.

CRUNCHY PEACH CAKE
Makes 9 servings

1 package (9 ounces) yellow cake mix *without* pudding in the mix
1 container (6 ounces) peach yogurt
1 egg
¼ cup peach all-fruit spread
¾ cup square whole-grain oat cereal with cinnamon, slightly crushed
  Whipped cream (optional)

1. Place oven rack in center of oven; preheat oven to 350°F. Lightly grease 8-inch square baking pan.

2. Beat cake mix, yogurt and egg in medium bowl with electric mixer at low speed about 1 minute or until blended. Increase speed to medium; beat 1 to 2 minutes or until smooth.

3. Spread batter in prepared pan. Drop fruit spread by ½ teaspoonfuls over cake batter. Sprinkle with cereal.

4. Bake about 25 minutes or until toothpick inserted into center comes out clean. Cool on wire rack. Serve with whipped cream, if desired.

If you use a glass baking dish instead of a metal one, reduce the oven temperature by 25°F.

TAFFY APPLE SNACK CAKE

Makes 9 servings

1 package (18¼ ounces) yellow cake mix with pudding in the mix, divided

2 eggs

¼ cup vegetable oil

¼ cup water

¼ cup packed brown sugar, divided

2 medium apples, peeled and diced

1 cup chopped nuts (optional)

2 tablespoons butter or margarine, melted

¼ teaspoon ground cinnamon

½ cup caramel topping

1. Preheat oven to 350°F. Spray 8-inch square baking pan with nonstick cooking spray. Reserve ¾ cup cake mix; set aside.

2. Pour remaining cake mix into large bowl. Add eggs, oil, water and 2 tablespoons brown sugar; beat with electric mixer at medium speed 2 minutes. Stir in apples; spread in prepared pan.

3. Combine reserved cake mix, remaining 2 tablespoons brown sugar, nuts, butter and cinnamon in medium bowl; mix until well blended. Sprinkle evenly over batter. Bake 40 to 45 minutes or until toothpick inserted into center comes out clean.

4. Cool cake in pan on wire rack. Cut into squares; top each serving with about 2 teaspoons caramel topping.

Taffy Apple Snack Cake

RICH TORTOISE CAKE

Makes 24 servings

1 package (18¼ ounces) devil's food cake mix, plus ingredients to prepare mix
1 cup chopped pecans
1 cup semisweet chocolate chips
½ teaspoon vanilla
½ cup prepared caramel sauce
    Additional chopped pecans and caramel sauce for garnish (optional)

1. Preheat oven to 350°F. Grease 13×9-inch baking pan.

2. Prepare cake mix according to package directions; stir 1 cup pecans, chocolate chips and vanilla into batter. Pour into prepared pan. Drizzle ½ cup caramel sauce over batter; swirl caramel into batter with knife.

3. Bake 35 to 40 minutes or until cake begins to pull away from sides of pan and toothpick inserted into center comes out clean. Cool to lukewarm on wire rack. Garnish each serving with additional pecans and caramel sauce, if desired.

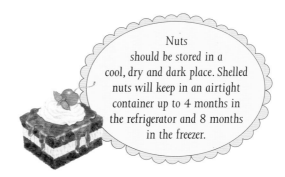

Nuts
should be stored in a
cool, dry and dark place. Shelled
nuts will keep in an airtight
container up to 4 months in
the refrigerator and 8 months
in the freezer.

CARROT SNACK CAKE

Makes 24 servings

1 package (18¼ ounces) butter recipe yellow cake mix with pudding in the mix, plus ingredients to prepare mix

2 jars (4 ounces each) strained carrot baby food

1 cup shredded carrots

1½ cups chopped walnuts, divided

½ cup golden raisins

1½ teaspoons ground cinnamon

1½ teaspoons vanilla, divided

1 package (8 ounces) cream cheese, softened

Grated peel of 1 lemon

2 teaspoons fresh lemon juice

3 cups powdered sugar

1. Preheat oven to 350°F. Grease 13×9-inch baking pan.

2. Prepare cake mix according to package directions but use only ½ cup water instead of amount directions call for. Stir baby food, carrots, 1 cup walnuts, raisins, cinnamon and ½ teaspoon vanilla into batter. Spread in prepared pan.

3. Bake 40 minutes or until cake begins to pull away from sides of pan and toothpick inserted into center comes out clean. Cool completely on wire rack before frosting.

4. Beat cream cheese in large bowl with electric mixer until fluffy. Beat in lemon peel, lemon juice and remaining 1 teaspoon vanilla. Gradually add powdered sugar, scraping down side of bowl occasionally; beat until well blended and smooth. Spread frosting over cooled cake; sprinkle with remaining ½ cup walnuts. Refrigerate 2 hours before cutting.

Cookie Jar Concoctions

CHOCOLATE GINGERSNAPS

Makes about 3 dozen cookies

¾ cup sugar
1 package (18¼ ounces) chocolate cake mix *without* pudding in the mix
1 tablespoon ground ginger
2 eggs
⅓ cup vegetable oil

1. Preheat oven to 350°F. Spray cookie sheets with nonstick cooking spray. Place sugar in shallow bowl.

2. Combine cake mix and ginger in large bowl. Add eggs and oil; stir until well blended.

3. Shape dough into 1-inch balls, using about 1 tablespoon dough for each cookie. Roll in sugar to coat. Place 2 inches apart on prepared cookie sheets.

4. Bake 10 minutes; transfer to wire racks to cool completely.

Chocolate Gingersnaps

CINNAMON CEREAL CRISPIES

Makes about 5 dozen cookies

½ cup granulated sugar

2 teaspoons ground cinnamon, divided

1 package (18¼ ounces) white or yellow cake mix with pudding in the mix

½ cup water

⅓ cup vegetable oil

1 egg

2 cups crisp rice cereal

1 cup cornflakes

1 cup raisins

1 cup chopped nuts (optional)

1. Preheat oven to 350°F. Lightly spray cookie sheets with nonstick cooking spray. Combine sugar and 1 teaspoon cinnamon in small bowl.

2. Beat cake mix, water, oil, egg and remaining 1 teaspoon cinnamon in large bowl with electric mixer at medium speed 1 minute. Gently stir in rice cereal, cornflakes, raisins and nuts until well blended.

3. Drop dough by rounded tablespoonfuls 2 inches apart onto prepared cookie sheets. Sprinkle lightly with cinnamon-sugar mixture.

4. Bake about 15 minutes or until lightly browned. Sprinkle cookies with additional cinnamon-sugar mixture after baking; transfer to wire racks to cool completely.

CRANBERRY GEMS

Makes about 5 dozen cookies

⅔ cup dried cranberries or dried cherries
½ cup granulated sugar
3 tablespoons water, divided
1 package (18¼ ounces) white cake mix with pudding in the mix
2 eggs
2 tablespoons vegetable oil
¼ teaspoon almond or vanilla extract
½ cup powdered sugar
1 to 2 teaspoons milk

1. Preheat oven to 350°F. Lightly grease cookie sheets.

2. Combine dried cranberries, granulated sugar and 1 tablespoon water in small microwavable bowl. Microwave at HIGH 1 minute; let cranberries stand 10 minutes before draining.

3. Blend cake mix, eggs, remaining 2 tablespoons water, oil and almond extract in large bowl until smooth. Drop dough by rounded teaspoonfuls 2 inches apart onto prepared cookie sheets. Top each cookie with several cranberries.

4. Bake 10 minutes or until edges are lightly browned. Top each cookie with another one or two cranberries after baking; transfer to wire racks to cool completely.

5. Blend powdered sugar and 1 teaspoon milk in small bowl until smooth. Add additional milk if necessary to reach pourable consistency. Drizzle glaze over cookies with tip of small spoon or fork.

MOON ROCKS

Makes about 3 dozen cookies

1 package (18¼ ounces) devil's food or German chocolate cake mix with pudding in the mix

3 eggs

½ cup (1 stick) butter, melted

2 cups slightly crushed (2½-inch) pretzel sticks

1½ cups uncooked old-fashioned oats

1 cup swirled chocolate and white chocolate chips or candy-coated chocolate baking pieces

1. Preheat oven to 350°F.

2. Blend cake mix, eggs and butter in large bowl. Stir in crushed pretzels, oats and chocolate chips. (Dough will be stiff.)

3. Drop dough by tablespoonfuls about 2 inches apart onto ungreased cookie sheets.

4. Bake about 12 minutes or until set. Let cookies stand on cookie sheets 1 minute; transfer to wire racks to to cool completely.

When melting butter in the microwave (about 1½ minutes for one stick), cover the container with a piece of waxed paper to prevent spatters.

QUICK FRUIT & LEMON DROPS

Makes about 2 dozen cookies

½ cup sugar
1 package (18¼ ounces) lemon cake mix
⅓ cup water
¼ cup butter, softened
1 egg
1 tablespoon grated lemon peel
1 cup mixed dried fruit bits

1. Preheat oven to 350°F. Grease cookie sheets. Place sugar in shallow bowl.

2. Beat cake mix, water, butter, egg and lemon peel in large bowl with electric mixer at low speed until well blended. Stir in fruit bits just until blended.

3. Shape dough into balls, using heaping tablespoon dough for each cookie. Roll in sugar to coat. Place 2 inches apart on prepared cookie sheets.

4. Bake 12 to 14 minutes or until set. Let cookies stand on cookie sheets 2 minutes; transfer to wire racks to cool completely.

NOTE: If dough is too sticky to handle, add about ¼ cup all-purpose flour.

BLACK AND WHITE SANDWICH COOKIES

Makes 3 dozen sandwich cookies

1 package (18¼ ounces) chocolate cake mix with pudding in the mix
1½ cups (3 sticks) unsalted butter, at room temperature, divided
2 egg yolks, divided
½ to ¾ cup milk, divided
1 package (18¼ ounces) butter recipe yellow cake mix with pudding in the mix
4 cups powdered sugar
¼ teaspoon salt

1. Preheat oven to 325°F. For chocolate cookies, place half of chocolate cake mix in large bowl. Add ½ cup butter; beat with electric mixer at high speed until well blended. Add 1 egg yolk and remaining cake mix; beat just until dough forms. Beat in 1 to 2 tablespoons milk if dough is too crumbly.

2. Shape dough into 36 balls, using about 1 tablespoon dough for each cookie. Place 2 inches apart on ungreased cookie sheets; flatten slightly. Bake 20 minutes or until cookies are firm. Let cookies stand on cookie sheets 5 minutes; transfer to wire racks to cool completely.

3. For vanilla cookies, place half of yellow cake mix in large bowl. Add ½ cup butter; beat with electric mixer at high speed until well blended. Add remaining egg yolk and cake mix; beat just until dough forms. Beat in 1 to 2 tablespoons milk if dough is too crumbly.

4. Shape dough into 36 balls, using about 1 tablespoon dough for each cookie. Place 2 inches apart on ungreased cookie sheets; flatten slightly. Bake 20 minutes or until cookies are firm. Let cookies stand on cookie sheets 5 minutes; transfer to wire racks to cool completely.

5. Cut remaining ½ cup butter into small pieces. Beat butter, powdered sugar, salt and 6 tablespoons milk in large bowl with electric mixer until light and fluffy. Add additional 2 tablespoons milk if necessary for more spreadable frosting.

6. Spread frosting on flat sides of chocolate cookies, using about 1 tablespoon per cookie. Top with vanilla cookies.

Cookie Jar Concoctions

PASTEL MINT SWIRLS

Makes 4 dozen cookies

⅓ **cup coarse or granulated sugar**
1 **package (18.25 ounces) devil's food cake mix** *without* **pudding in the mix**
3 **eggs**
¼ **cup butter, melted**
¼ **cup unsweetened cocoa powder**
144 **small or 48 large pastel mint chips**

1. Preheat oven to 375°F. Place sugar in shallow bowl.

2. Combine cake mix, eggs, butter and cocoa in large bowl just until blended. (Dough will be stiff.)

3. Shape dough into 1-inch balls; roll in sugar to coat. Place 2 inches apart on ungreased cookie sheets.

4. Bake 8 to 9 minutes or until tops are cracked. Gently press 3 small or 1 large mint into top of each cookie. Let cookies stand on cookie sheets 1 minute; transfer to wire racks to cool completely.

CHOCOLATE CHIP OAT COOKIES

Makes 4 dozen cookies

1 package (18¼ ounces) yellow cake mix
1 teaspoon baking powder
¾ cup vegetable oil
2 eggs
1 teaspoon vanilla
1 cup uncooked old-fashioned oats
¾ cup semisweet chocolate chips

1. Preheat oven to 350°F. Lightly grease cookie sheets or line with parchment paper.

2. Combine cake mix and baking powder in large bowl. Add oil, eggs and vanilla; beat by hand until well blended. Stir in oats and chocolate chips.

3. Drop dough by slightly rounded tablespoonfuls 2 inches apart onto prepared cookie sheets. Bake 10 minutes or until golden brown. *Do not overbake.*

4. Let cookies stand on cookie sheets 5 minutes; transfer to wire racks to cool completely.

SUNSHINE SANDWICHES

Makes 2½ dozen cookies

⅓ cup coarse or granulated sugar
¾ cup (1½ sticks) plus 2 tablespoons butter, softened, divided
1 egg
2 tablespoons grated lemon peel
1 package (18¼ ounces) lemon cake mix with pudding in the mix
¼ cup yellow cornmeal
2 cups sifted powdered sugar
2 to 3 tablespoons lemon juice
Yellow food coloring

1. Preheat oven to 375°F. Place coarse sugar in shallow bowl.

2. Beat ¾ cup butter in large bowl with electric mixer at medium speed until fluffy. Add egg and lemon peel; beat 30 seconds. Add cake mix, ⅓ at a time, beating at low speed after each addition until combined. Stir in cornmeal. (Dough will be stiff.)

3. Shape dough into 1-inch balls; roll in sugar to coat. Place 2 inches apart on ungreased cookie sheets.

4. Bake 8 to 9 minutes or until bottoms begin to brown. Let cookies stand on cookie sheets 1 minute; transfer to wire racks to cool completely.

5. Meanwhile, beat powdered sugar and remaining 2 tablespoons butter in small bowl with electric mixer at low speed until blended. Gradually add enough lemon juice to reach spreading consistency. Stir in food coloring to reach desired shade of yellow.

6. Spread 1 slightly rounded teaspoon frosting on bottom of one cookie. Top with second cookie, bottom side down. Repeat with remaining cookies and frosting. Store covered at room temperature for up to 24 hours or freeze.

GARBAGE PAIL COOKIES

Makes about 3 dozen cookies

1 package (18¼ ounces) white cake mix with pudding in the mix
½ cup (1 stick) unsalted butter, at room temperature
2 eggs
1 teaspoon vanilla
1 teaspoon ground cinnamon
½ cup mini candy-coated chocolate pieces
½ cup salted peanuts
½ cup peanut butter chips
1½ cups crushed salted potato chips

1. Preheat oven to 350°F. Lightly grease cookie sheets.

2. Beat half of cake mix, butter, eggs, vanilla and cinnamon in large bowl with electric mixer at medium speed until light. Beat in remaining cake mix until well blended. Stir in candy-coated chocolate pieces, peanuts and peanut butter chips. Stir in potato chips. (Dough will be stiff.)

3. Drop dough by rounded tablespoonfuls 2 inches apart onto prepared cookie sheets.

4. Bake 15 to 17 minutes or until golden brown. Let cookies stand on cookie sheets 2 minutes; transfer to wire racks to cool completely.

CHOCOLATE HAZELNUT COOKIES

Makes 4 dozen cookies

$\frac{1}{2}$ **cup chopped pecans**
1 package (8 ounces) cream cheese, softened
$\frac{1}{2}$ **cup (1 stick) butter, softened**
1 egg
1 package (18$\frac{1}{4}$ ounces) devil's food cake mix
1 jar (12 ounces) chocolate hazelnut spread
$\frac{1}{4}$ **cup powdered sugar**

1. Preheat oven 350°F.

2. Place pecans in small resealable plastic bag. Finely crush pecans using meat mallet or rolling pin. Place pecans in small skillet over medium-high heat; cook $1\frac{1}{2}$ minutes or until browned, stirring constantly. Remove from heat; set aside.

3. Beat cream cheese and butter with electric mixer at low speed 30 seconds or until smooth. Add egg; beat at medium speed until well blended. Add cake mix; beat at low speed 2 minutes or until mixture is smooth and resembles thick cookie dough. Stir in toasted pecans.

4. Shape dough into 1-inch balls. (Lightly spray palms with cooking spray if necessary to make handling dough easier.) Place balls 1 inch apart on ungreased cookie sheets.

5. Bake 8 minutes. (Cookies will appear underbaked.) Let cookies stand on cookie sheets 5 minutes; transfer to wire racks to cool completely.

6. Spoon 1 teaspoon chocolate hazelnut spread over each cookie; sprinkle with powdered sugar.

SWEET MYSTERIES

Makes 3 dozen cookies

  1 package (18¼ ounces) yellow cake mix with pudding in the mix
½ cup (1 stick) unsalted butter, at room temperature
  1 egg
  1 cup ground pecans
36 milk chocolate candy kisses
    Powdered sugar

1. Preheat oven to 325°F.

2. Beat half of cake mix and butter in large bowl with electric mixer at high speed until light. Add egg and remaining cake mix; beat at medium speed just until dough forms. Add pecans; beat just until blended.

3. Shape rounded tablespoonful dough around each candy, making sure candy is completely covered. Place cookies 1 inch apart on ungreased cookie sheets.

4. Bake 18 to 20 minutes or until firm and just beginning to turn golden brown. Let cookies stand on cookie sheets 10 minutes. Transfer to wire racks set over waxed paper; dust with powdered sugar.

Bar Cookie Bonanza

GRANOLA RAISIN BARS

Makes 15 bars

   1 package (18¼ ounces) yellow cake mix with pudding in the mix, divided
   ½ cup (1 stick) butter or margarine, melted, divided
   1 egg
   4 cups granola cereal with raisins

1. Preheat oven to 350°F. Lightly spray 13×9-inch baking pan with nonstick cooking spray. Reserve ½ cup cake mix; set aside.

2. Combine remaining cake mix, 4 tablespoons melted butter and egg in large bowl; stir until well blended. (Dough will be thick and sticky.) Spoon dough into prepared pan. Cover with plastic wrap and press dough evenly into pan, using plastic wrap to keep hands from sticking to dough.

3. Bake 8 minutes. Meanwhile, combine reserved cake mix, granola cereal and remaining 4 tablespoons melted butter in medium bowl; stir until well blended. Spread mixture evenly over partially baked bars.

4. Return pan to oven; bake 15 to 20 minutes or until edges are lightly browned. Cool completely in pan on wire rack.

Granola Raisin Bars

ICE CREAM SANDWICHES

Makes 8 sandwiches

1 package (18¼ ounces) chocolate cake mix with pudding in the mix
2 eggs
¼ cup warm water
3 tablespoons butter or margarine, melted
1 pint vanilla ice cream, softened
Decorative sugar or colored sprinkles

1. Preheat oven to 350°F. Lightly spray 13×9-inch pan with nonstick cooking spray. Line pan with aluminum foil and spray again.

2. Beat cake mix, eggs, water and melted butter in large bowl with electric mixer until well blended. (Dough will be thick and sticky.) Spoon dough into prepared pan. Cover with plastic wrap and press dough evenly into pan, using plastic wrap to keep hands from sticking to dough. Remove plastic wrap and prick surface all over with fork (about 40 times) to prevent dough from rising too much.

3. Bake 20 minutes or until toothpick inserted into center comes out clean. Cool in pan on wire rack.

4. Cut cookie in half crosswise; remove one half from pan. Spread ice cream evenly over cookie half remaining in pan. Top with second half; use foil in pan to wrap up sandwich.

5. Freeze at least 4 hours. Cut into 8 equal pieces; dip cut ends in sugar or sprinkles. Wrap and freeze sandwiches until ready to serve.

PEPPERMINT ICE CREAM SANDWICHES: Stir ⅓ cup crushed peppermint candies into vanilla ice cream before assembling. Roll ends of sandwiches in additional crushed peppermint candies to coat.

TIP: If the ice cream is too hard to scoop easily, microwave at HIGH 10 seconds to soften.

PEANUT BUTTER CHEESECAKE BARS

Makes 2 dozen bars or triangles

1 package (18¼ ounces) yellow cake mix with pudding in the mix
½ cup (1 stick) unsalted butter, at room temperature, cut into small pieces
2 packages (8 ounces each) cream cheese, at room temperature
1 cup chunky peanut butter
3 eggs
1¼ cups sugar
1 cup salted roasted peanuts, coarsely chopped
Melted chocolate (optional)

1. Preheat oven to 325°F.

2. Beat cake mix and butter in large bowl with electric mixer at medium speed just until crumbly. Reserve 1 cup mixture. Press remaining mixture evenly into ungreased 13×9-inch baking pan to form crust. Bake 10 minutes; cool on wire rack.

3. Beat cream cheese and peanut butter in large bowl with electric mixer at medium speed until fluffy. Beat in eggs, one at a time, scraping down side of bowl occasionally. Gradually beat in sugar until light. Spread filling over cooled crust.

4. Combine reserved cake mix mixture and peanuts; sprinkle evenly over filling.

5. Bake 45 minutes or until just set and knife inserted into cheesecake layer comes out clean. Remove from oven; cool at room temperature 30 minutes. Chill at least 2 hours before serving. Drizzle with melted chocolate, if desired.

BURIED CHERRY BARS

Makes 2 dozen bars

1 jar (10 ounces) maraschino cherries

1 package (18¼ ounces) devil's food cake mix *without* pudding in the mix

1 cup (2 sticks) butter, melted

1 egg

½ teaspoon almond extract

1½ cups semisweet chocolate chips

¾ cup sweetened condensed milk

½ cup chopped pecans

1. Preheat oven to 350°F. Lightly grease 13×9-inch baking pan. Drain maraschino cherries, reserving 2 tablespoons juice. Cut cherries into quarters.

2. Combine cake mix, butter, egg and almond extract in large bowl; mix well. (Batter will be very thick.) Spread batter in prepared pan. Lightly press cherries into batter.

3. Combine chocolate chips and sweetened condensed milk in small saucepan. Cook over low heat, stirring constantly, until chocolate melts. Stir in reserved cherry juice. Spread chocolate mixture over cherries in pan; sprinkle with pecans.

4. Bake 35 to 40 minutes or until almost set in center. Cool completely on wire rack.

Store leftover sweetened condensed milk in an airtight container in the refrigerator for up to 5 days.

CHOCOLATE & OAT TOFFEE BARS

Makes 2½ dozen bars

¾ cup (1½ sticks) plus 2 tablespoons unsalted butter, at room temperature
1 package (18¼ ounces) yellow cake mix with pudding in the mix
2 cups uncooked quick-cooking oats
¼ cup packed brown sugar
1 egg
½ teaspoon vanilla
1 cup toffee chips
½ cup chopped pecans
⅓ cup semisweet chocolate chips

1. Preheat oven to 350°F. Grease 13×9-inch baking pan.

2. Beat ¾ cup butter in large bowl with electric mixer until creamy. Add cake mix, oats, brown sugar, egg and vanilla; beat 1 minute or until well blended. Stir in toffee chips and pecans. Pat dough into prepared pan.

3. Bake 31 to 35 minutes or until golden brown. Cool completely in pan on wire rack.

4. Melt remaining 2 tablespoons butter and chocolate chips in small saucepan over very low heat. Drizzle warm glaze over bars. Let glaze set 1 hour at room temperature. Cut into bars with sharp knife.

Chocolate & Oat Toffee Bars

JAM JAM BARS

Makes 24 bars

1 package (18¼ ounces) yellow or white cake mix with pudding
    in the mix

½ cup (1 stick) butter or margarine, melted

1 cup apricot preserves or raspberry jam

1 package (11 ounces) peanut butter and milk chocolate chips

1. Preheat oven to 350°F. Lightly spray 13×9-inch baking pan with nonstick cooking spray.

2. Pour cake mix into large bowl; stir in melted butter until well blended. (Dough will be lumpy.) Remove ½ cup dough and set aside. Press remaining dough evenly into prepared pan. Spread preserves in thin layer over dough in pan.

3. Place chips in medium bowl. Stir in reserved dough until well mixed. (Dough will remain in small lumps evenly distributed throughout chips.) Sprinkle mixture evenly over preserves.

4. Bake about 30 minutes or until lightly browned and bubbling at edges. Cool completely in pan on wire rack.

LEMON CHEESE BARS

Makes 1 ½ dozen bars

1 package (18¼ ounces) white or yellow cake mix with pudding
    in the mix
2 eggs, divided
⅓ cup vegetable oil
1 package (8 ounces) cream cheese
⅓ cup sugar
1 teaspoon lemon juice

1. Preheat oven to 350°F.

2. Combine cake mix, 1 egg and oil in large bowl; stir until crumbly.
Reserve 1 cup crumb mixture. Press remaining crumb mixture into ungreased
13×9-inch baking pan. Bake 15 minutes or until light golden brown.

3. Meanwhile, combine remaining egg, cream cheese, sugar and lemon juice
in medium bowl; beat until smooth and well blended. Spread over baked crust.
Sprinkle with reserved crumb mixture.

4. Bake 15 minutes or until cream cheese layer is just set. Cool in pan on wire
rack.

CHOCOLATE PEANUT BUTTER CANDY BARS

Makes 2 dozen bars

1 package (18¼ ounces) devil's food or dark chocolate cake mix without pudding in the mix

1 can (5 ounces) evaporated milk

⅓ cup butter, melted

½ cup dry-roasted peanuts

4 packages (1½ ounces each) chocolate peanut butter cups, coarsely chopped

1. Preheat oven to 350°F. Lightly grease 13×9-inch baking pan.

2. Beat cake mix, evaporated milk and butter in large bowl with electric mixer at medium speed until well blended. (Dough will be stiff.) Spread ⅔ of dough in prepared pan. Sprinkle with peanuts.

3. Bake 10 minutes; remove from oven and sprinkle with chopped candy.

4. Drop remaining dough by small spoonfuls over candy. Bake 15 to 20 minutes or until set. Cool completely on wire rack.

*Make sure to use evaporated milk in this recipe, **not** sweetened condensed milk— these two products are not interchangeable.*

FRUIT-LAYERED CHEESECAKE BARS

Makes 16 bars

1 package (18¼ ounces) yellow cake mix
½ cup (1 stick) butter, softened
2 eggs
3 tablespoons water
2 packages (8 ounces each) cream cheese, softened
1 cup powdered sugar
¼ cup milk
2 teaspoons vanilla
1 can (8 ounces) pineapple tidbits, drained and juice reserved
3 tablespoons orange juice
¾ teaspoon cornstarch
1 medium banana (about 6 ounces), peeled and thinly sliced
1 cup fresh mango or nectarine pieces
1 pint whole strawberries, quartered

1. Preheat oven to 350°F. Grease 13×9-inch baking pan.

2. Beat cake mix, butter, eggs and water in large bowl with electric mixer at low speed 1 to 2 minutes or until stiff dough forms. Press dough evenly onto bottom of prepared pan.

3. Bake 27 minutes or until toothpick inserted into center comes out clean. Cool completely in pan on wire rack.

4. Meanwhile, beat cream cheese, sugar, milk and vanilla with electric mixer at low speed 30 seconds or until just blended. Beat 1 minute on high speed or until smooth.

5. Combine reserved pineapple juice, orange juice and cornstarch in small saucepan; stir until cornstarch is completely dissolved. Cook and stir over medium heat until mixture comes to a boil; cook and stir 1 minute. Remove from heat; cool completely.

6. Spread cream cheese mixture evenly over baked crust; arrange pineapple, banana, mango and strawberries on top. Spoon or brush pineapple juice mixture over fruit. Cover with plastic wrap; refrigerate 1 hour or up to 24 hours before serving.

Fruit-Layered Cheesecake Bars

OOEY-GOOEY CARAMEL PEANUT BUTTER BARS

Makes 2 dozen bars

1 package (18¼ ounces) yellow cake mix *without* pudding in the mix
1 cup uncooked quick-cooking oats
⅔ cup creamy peanut butter
1 egg, slightly beaten
2 tablespoons milk
1 package (8 ounces) cream cheese, softened
1 jar (12¼ ounces) caramel ice cream topping
1 cup semisweet chocolate chips

1. Preheat oven to 350°F. Lightly grease 13×9-inch baking pan.

2. Combine cake mix and oats in large bowl. Cut in peanut butter with pastry blender or 2 knives until mixture is crumbly.

3. Blend egg and milk in small bowl. Add to peanut butter mixture; stir just until combined. Reserve 1 cup mixture. Press remaining peanut butter mixture into prepared pan.

4. Beat cream cheese with electric mixer at medium speed until fluffy. Add caramel topping; beat just until blended. Carefully spread over peanut butter layer in pan.

5. Break up reserved peanut butter mixture into small pieces; sprinkle over cream cheese layer. Top with chocolate chips.

6. Bake about 30 minutes or until almost set in center. Cool completely in pan on wire rack.

Crazy for Cupcakes

MINI DOUGHNUT CUPCAKES

Makes about 48 cupcakes

    1 cup sugar
1½ teaspoons ground cinnamon
    1 package (18¼ ounces) yellow or white cake mix, plus ingredients to
        prepare mix
    1 tablespoon ground nutmeg

1. Preheat oven to 350°F. Grease and flour 24 mini (1¾-inch) muffin pan cups. Combine sugar and cinnamon in small bowl; set aside.

2. Prepare cake mix according to package directions; stir nutmeg into batter. Fill muffin cups ⅔ full.

3. Bake about 12 minutes or until lightly browned and toothpick inserted into centers comes out clean.

4. Remove cupcakes from pans; roll in sugar mixture until completely coated. Serve warm or at room temperature.

TIP: Save any remaining cinnamon sugar mixture to sprinkle on toast and pancakes.

Mini Doughnut Cupcakes

MARSHMALLOW FUDGE SUNDAE CUPCAKES

Makes 20 cupcakes

1 package (18¼ ounces) chocolate cake mix, plus ingredients to
    prepare mix
2 packages (4 ounces each) waffle bowls
40 marshmallows
1 jar (8 ounces) hot fudge topping
1¼ cups whipped topping
¼ cup colored sprinkles
1 jar (10 ounces) maraschino cherries

1. Preheat oven to 350°F. Lightly spray 20 standard (2½-inch) muffin pan cups with nonstick cooking spray.

2. Prepare cake mix according to package directions. Fill muffin cups about ⅔ full.

3. Bake about 20 minutes or until toothpick inserted into centers comes out clean. Cool in pans on wire racks about 10 minutes.

4. Remove cupcakes from pans and place one cupcake in each waffle bowl. Place waffle bowls on baking sheet. Top each cupcake with 2 marshmallows; return to oven 2 minutes or until marshmallows are slightly softened.

5. Remove lid from fudge topping; microwave at HIGH 10 seconds or until softened. Spoon 2 teaspoons fudge topping over each cupcake. Top with 1 tablespoon whipped topping, sprinkles and cherry.

MISS PINKY THE PIG CUPCAKES

Makes 24 cupcakes

2 jars (10 ounces each) maraschino cherries, stemmed and well drained

1 package (18¼ ounces) white cake mix *without* pudding in the mix

1 cup sour cream

½ cup vegetable oil

3 egg whites

¼ cup water

½ teaspoon almond extract

Red food coloring

1 container (16 ounces) cream cheese frosting

48 small gum drops

Mini candy-coated chocolate pieces, mini chocolate chips, white decorating icing and colored sugar

1. Preheat oven to 350°F. Line 24 standard (2½-inch) muffin pan cups with paper liners. Spray 24 mini (1¾-inch) muffin pan cups with nonstick cooking spray. Pat cherries dry with paper towels. Place in food processor; process 4 to 5 seconds or until finely chopped.

2. Beat cake mix, sour cream, oil, egg whites, water and almond extract in large bowl with electric mixer at low speed about 1 minute or until blended. Increase speed to medium; beat 1 to 2 minutes or until smooth. Stir in cherries.

3. Spoon about 2 slightly rounded tablespoons batter into prepared standard muffin cups, filling each about ½ full. (Cups will be slightly less full than normal.) Spoon remaining batter into mini muffin cups, filling each about ⅓ full.

4. Bake standard cupcakes 14 to 18 minutes and mini cupcakes 7 to 9 minutes or until toothpick inserted into centers comes out clean. Cool cupcakes in pans on wire racks 5 minutes; remove from pans and cool completely on wire racks. Remove paper liners from larger cupcakes.

5. Add food coloring to frosting, a few drops at a time, until desired color is reached. Frost tops of larger cupcakes with pink frosting. Gently press small cupcake onto one side of each large cupcake top. Frost tops and sides of small cupcakes.

6. Place gumdrops between two layers of waxed paper. Flatten to ⅛-inch thickness with rolling pin; cut out triangles. Arrange gumdrop ears on cupcakes; complete faces with chocolate candies, chocolate chips, white icing and colored sugar.

TROPICAL LUAU CUPCAKES

Makes 30 cupcakes

2 cans (8 ounces each) crushed pineapple in juice
1 package (18¼ ounces) yellow cake mix *without* pudding in the mix
1 package (4-serving size) banana cream-flavor instant pudding and
   pie filling mix
4 eggs
⅓ cup vegetable oil
¼ teaspoon ground nutmeg
1 container (12 ounces) whipped vanilla frosting
¾ cup flaked coconut, toasted
3 to 4 medium kiwi
30 (2½-inch) pretzel sticks

1. Preheat oven to 350°F. Line 30 standard (2½-inch) muffin pan cups with paper liners. Drain pineapple, reserving juice. Set pineapple aside.

2. Beat reserved pineapple juice, cake mix, pudding mix, eggs, oil and nutmeg in large bowl with electric mixer at low speed 1 minute or until blended. Increase speed to medium; beat 1 to 2 minutes or until smooth. Fold in pineapple. Fill muffin cups ⅔ full.

3. Bake about 20 minutes or until toothpick inserted into centers comes out clean. Cool cupcakes in pans on wire racks 5 minutes; remove from pans and cool completely on wire racks.

4. Frost cupcakes with frosting; sprinkle with coconut. For palm trees*, peel kiwi and cut into ⅛-inch-thick slices. Create palm fronds by cutting each slice at ⅜-inch intervals, cutting from outside edge toward center. (Leave about ¾- to 1-inch circle uncut in center of each slice). For palm tree trunk, push pretzel stick into, but not through, center of each kiwi slice. Push other end of pretzel into top of each cupcake.

*Palm tree decorations can be made up to 1 hour before serving.

TIP: To toast coconut, spread evenly on ungreased baking sheet; bake in preheated 350°F oven 4 to 6 minutes or until light golden brown, stirring frequently.

CUBCAKES

Makes 24 cupcakes

  1 package (18¼ ounces) chocolate cake mix, plus ingredients to
     prepare mix
  1 container (16 ounces) chocolate frosting
  1 package (5 ounces) chocolate nonpareil candies
72 red cinnamon candies
    Chocolate sprinkles
    Black decorating gel

1. Line 24 standard (2½-inch) muffin pan cups with paper liners or spray with nonstick cooking spray.

2. Prepare cake mix and bake in prepared pans according to package directions. Cool cupcakes in pans on wire racks 15 minutes; remove from pans and cool completely on wire racks.

3. Frost cooled cupcakes with chocolate frosting. Use nonpareil candies to create ears and muzzles. Add cinnamon candies for eyes and noses; decorate with chocolate sprinkles for fur. Use decorating gel to place dots on eyes and create mouth.

To fill muffin cups
neatly and easily, place the
batter in a 4-cup glass measure.
Use a plastic spatula to control the
flow of the batter.

CARROT CREAM CHEESE CUPCAKES

Makes 14 cupcakes

1 package (8 ounces) cream cheese, softened
¼ cup powdered sugar
1 package (18¼ ounces) spice cake mix, plus ingredients to prepare mix
2 cups grated carrots
2 tablespoons finely chopped candied ginger (optional)
1 container (16 ounces) cream cheese frosting
3 tablespoons maple syrup
   Orange peel strips for garnish (optional)

1. Preheat oven to 350°F. Line 14 large (3½-inch) muffin pan cups with paper or foil liners.

2. Beat cream cheese and powdered sugar in large bowl with electric mixer at medium speed 1 minute or until light and fluffy. Cover and refrigerate until needed.

3. Prepare cake mix according to package directions; stir carrots and ginger into batter.

4. Fill muffin cups ⅓ full (about ¼ cup batter). Place 1 tablespoon cream cheese mixture in center of each cup. Top with remaining batter (muffin cups should be ⅔ full).

5. Bake 25 to 28 minutes or until toothpick inserted into centers comes out clean. Cool cupcakes in pans on wire racks 10 minutes; remove from pans and cool completely on wire racks.

6. Mix frosting and maple syrup until well blended. Frost tops of cupcakes; decorate with orange peel, if desired.

DOODLE BUG CUPCAKES

Makes 24 cupcakes

1 package (18¼ ounces) white cake mix *without* pudding in the mix
1 cup sour cream
3 eggs
⅓ cup vegetable oil
⅓ cup water
1 teaspoon vanilla
1½ cups prepared cream cheese frosting
    Red, yellow, blue and green food coloring
    Red licorice strings, cut into 2-inch pieces
    Assorted round decorating candies

1. Preheat oven to 350°F. Line 24 standard (2½-inch) muffin pan cups with paper liners.

2. Beat cake mix, sour cream, eggs, oil, water and vanilla in large bowl with electric mixer at low speed about 1 minute or until blended. Increase speed to medium; beat 1 to 2 minutes or until smooth.

3. Fill muffin cups about ⅔ full. Bake about 20 minutes or until toothpick inserted into centers comes out clean.

4. Cool cupcakes in pans on wire racks 5 minutes; remove from pans and cool completely on wire racks.

5. Divide frosting equally between 4 small bowls. Add food coloring to each bowl, one drop at a time, to reach desired colors; stir each frosting until well blended. Frost tops of cupcakes.

6. Use toothpick or wooden skewer to make three small holes on opposite sides of each cupcake. Insert licorice piece into each hole for legs. Decorate tops of cupcakes with assorted candies.

FUDGY CUPCAKES WITH CHOCOLATE GANACHE

Makes 18 cupcakes

1 package (18¼ ounces) devil's food cake mix *without* pudding in the mix
1 package (4-serving size) chocolate fudge-flavor instant pudding and
   pie filling mix
1⅓ cups water
3 eggs
½ cup vegetable oil
6 ounces semisweet chocolate, finely chopped
½ cup heavy whipping cream
White decorating icing

1. Preheat oven to 350°F. Line 18 standard (2½-inch) muffin pan cups with paper liners.

2. Beat cake mix, pudding mix, water, eggs and oil in large bowl with electric mixer at medium speed 2 minutes or until well blended. Fill muffin cups ⅔ full.

3. Bake 22 to 24 minutes or until toothpick inserted into centers comes out clean. Cool cupcakes in pans on wire racks 10 minutes; remove from pans and cool completely on wire racks.

4. To prepare ganache, place chocolate in small bowl. Heat cream in small saucepan over medium-low heat until bubbles appear around edge of pan. Pour cream over chocolate; let stand about 2 minutes. Stir until mixture is smooth and shiny. Allow ganache to cool completely. (It will be slightly runny.)

5. Dip tops of cupcakes into chocolate ganache; smooth surface. Let ganache set 20 minutes.

6. Pipe letters onto cupcakes with white decorating icing.

HIS AND HER CUPCAKES

Makes 24 cupcakes

  1 package (18¼ ounces) cake mix, any flavor, plus ingredients to
     prepare mix
  1 container (16 ounces) vanilla frosting
  3 rolls (¾ ounce each) fruit leather, cut into 4×2⅜-inch strips
12 pieces striped fruit gum
     Red food coloring
24 vanilla wafer cookies
     Small candies

1. Line 24 standard (2½-inch) muffin pan cups with paper liners or spray with nonstick cooking spray.

2. Prepare cake mix and bake in prepared pans according to package directions. Cool cupcakes in pans on wire racks 15 minutes; remove from pans and cool completely on wire racks.

3. For "His" cupcakes, frost 12 cupcakes. Place 1 strip fruit leather on each frosted cupcake to form shirt collar. Cut gum into tie shapes and place on cupcakes.

4. Add food coloring to remaining frosting, a few drops at a time, until desired shade of pink is reached; stir until well blended.

5. For "Her" cupcakes, frost remaining cupcakes with pink frosting. Use dab of frosting to sandwich two vanilla wafer cookies together. Repeat with remaining cookies. Frost cookie sandwiches pink. Top each cupcake with frosted cookie sandwich, placing slightly off-center for crown of hat. Decorate hats with fruit leather and candies.

LAZY DAISY CUPCAKES

Makes 24 cupcakes

1 package (18¼ ounces) yellow cake mix, plus ingredients to prepare mix
   Yellow food coloring
1 container (16 ounces) vanilla frosting
30 marshmallows
24 small round candies or gumdrops

1. Line 24 standard (2½-inch) muffin pan cups with paper liners or spray with nonstick cooking spray.

2. Prepare cake mix and bake in prepared pans according to package directions. Cool cupcakes in pans on wire racks 15 minutes; remove from pans and cool completely on wire racks.

3. Add food coloring to frosting, a few drops at a time, until desired shade of yellow is reached. Frost cupcakes with yellow frosting.

4. Cut each marshmallow crosswise into 4 pieces with scissors. Stretch pieces into petal shapes; place 5 pieces on each cupcake to form flower. Place candy in center of each flower.

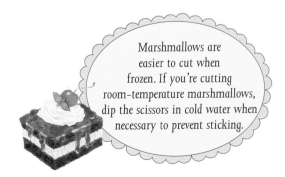

Marshmallows are easier to cut when frozen. If you're cutting room-temperature marshmallows, dip the scissors in cold water when necessary to prevent sticking.

CHOCOLATE CHERRY CUPCAKES

Makes 22 cupcakes

1 package (18¼ ounces) devil's food cake mix *without* pudding in the mix
1⅓ cups water
3 eggs
½ cup sour cream
⅓ cup oil
1 cup dried cherries
1 container (16 ounces) vanilla frosting, divided
   Green food coloring
11 maraschino cherries, stemmed and cut into halves

1. Preheat oven to 350°F. Line 22 standard (2½-inch) muffin pan cups with paper liners.

2. Beat cake mix, water, eggs, sour cream and oil in large bowl with electric mixer at low speed 30 seconds or until just blended. Beat at medium speed 2 minutes or until smooth. Fold in dried cherries. Fill muffin cups ¾ full.

3. Bake 20 to 24 minutes or until toothpick inserted into centers comes out clean. Cool cupcakes in pans on wire racks 10 minutes; remove from pans and cool completely on wire racks.

4. Place ¼ cup frosting in small bowl; stir in food coloring, one drop at a time, until desired shade of green is reached. Stir until well blended.

5. Frost cupcakes with remaining white frosting. Place 1 maraschino cherry half, cut side down, onto each cupcake. Place green frosting in pastry bag fitted with writing tip. Pipe stem and leaf onto each cupcake.

WHITE CHOCOLATE MACADAMIA CUPCAKES

Makes 20 cupcakes

1 package (18¼ ounces) white cake mix *without* pudding in the mix, plus
   ingredients to prepare mix
1 package (4-serving size) white chocolate-flavor instant pudding and
   pie filling mix
¾ cup chopped macadamia nuts
1½ cups flaked coconut
1 cup white chocolate chips
1 container (16 ounces) white frosting

1. Preheat oven to 350°F. Line 20 standard (2½-inch) muffin pan cups with paper liners.

2. Prepare cake mix according to package directions, beating in pudding mix with cake mix ingredients. Fold in nuts. Fill muffin cups ⅔ full.

3. Bake 18 to 20 minutes or until toothpick inserted into centers comes out clean. Cool cupcakes in pans on wire racks 10 minutes; remove from pans and cool completely on wire racks.

4. Meanwhile, spread coconut evenly on ungreased baking sheet; bake at 350°F 6 minutes, stirring occasionally, until light golden brown. Cool completely.

5. Place white chocolate chips in small microwavable bowl; microwave 2 minutes at MEDIUM (50% power), stirring every 30 seconds, until melted and smooth. Cool slightly before stirring into frosting.

6. Frost cupcakes; sprinkle with toasted coconut.

BUTTERFLY CUPCAKES

Makes 24 cupcakes

1 package (18¼ ounces) cake mix, any flavor, plus ingredients to prepare mix
1 container (16 ounces) vanilla frosting
Blue and green food coloring
Assorted candies and colored sugar
Red licorice ropes, cut into 4-inch pieces

1. Preheat oven to 350°F. Lightly spray 24 standard (2½-inch) muffin pan cups with nonstick cooking spray.

2. Prepare cake mix according to package directions. Fill muffin cups about ⅔ full.

3. Bake about 20 minutes or until toothpick inserted into centers comes out clean. Cool cupcakes in pans on wire racks about 10 minutes; remove from pans and cool completely on wire racks.

4. Divide frosting equally between 2 small bowls. Add food coloring to each bowl, one drop at a time, to reach desired colors; stir each frosting until well blended.

5. Cut cupcakes in half. Place cupcake halves together, cut sides out, to resemble butterfly wings. Frost with desired color; decorate with candies and colored sugar as shown in photo. Snip each end of licorice rope pieces to form antennae; place in center of each cupcake.

PEANUT BUTTER & MILK CHOCOLATE CUPCAKES

Makes 24 cupcakes

1 package (18¼ ounces) butter recipe yellow cake mix with pudding in the mix, plus ingredients to prepare mix
½ cup creamy peanut butter
2 bars (3½ ounces each) good-quality milk chocolate, broken into small pieces
¼ cup (½ stick) unsalted butter, cut into small chunks
¼ cup heavy cream
   Dash salt
   Peanut butter chips (optional)

1. Preheat oven to 350°F. Line 24 standard (2½-inch) muffin pan cups with paper liners.

2. Prepare cake mix according to package directions but use ¼ cup butter instead of ½ cup directions call for, and beat in peanut butter with butter. Fill muffin cups evenly with batter.

3. Bake 24 to 26 minutes or until light golden brown and toothpick inserted into centers comes out clean. Cool cupcakes in pans on wire racks 5 minutes; remove from pans and cool completely on wire racks.

4. Combine chocolate, butter, cream and salt in small heavy saucepan. Heat over very low heat, stirring constantly, just until butter and chocolate melt. Mixture should be tepid, not hot.

5. Immediately spoon about 1 tablespoon chocolate glaze over each cupcake, spreading to cover top. Sprinkle with peanut butter chips, if desired.

LEMON-UP CAKES

Makes 24 cupcakes

  1 package (18¼ ounces) white cake mix with pudding in the mix, plus
      ingredients to prepare mix
  ½ cup fresh lemon juice, divided (2 large lemons)
      Grated peel of 2 lemons, divided
  ½ cup (1 stick) butter, at room temperature
  3½ cups powdered sugar
      Yellow food coloring
  1 package (9½ ounces) lemon-shaped candies, coarsely crushed

1. Preheat oven to 350°F. Line 24 standard (2½-inch) muffin pan cups with paper liners.

2. Prepare cake mix according to package directions but use ¼ cup less water than directions call for. Stir in ¼ cup lemon juice and half of grated lemon peel. Fill muffin cups evenly with batter.

3. Bake 23 minutes or until light golden brown and toothpick inserted into centers comes out clean. Cool cupcakes in pans on wire racks 5 minutes; remove from pans and cool completely on wire racks.

4. Beat butter in large bowl with electric mixer at medium speed until creamy. Gradually add powdered sugar to form stiff mixture. Add remaining ¼ cup lemon juice, lemon peel and several drops food coloring; beat at high speed until frosting is light and fluffy.

5. Generously frost cupcakes. Sprinkle crushed candies over frosting.

PUPCAKES

Makes 24 cupcakes

1 package (18¼ ounces) chocolate cake mix, plus ingredients to
    prepare mix
½ cup (1 stick) unsalted butter, at room temperature
4 cups powdered sugar
¼ to ½ cup half-and-half or milk
    Red and yellow fruit roll-ups
    Assorted colored jelly beans and candy-coated chocolate pieces

1. Preheat oven to 350°F. Line 24 standard (2½-inch) muffin pan cups with paper liners.

2. Prepare cake mix and bake in prepared pans according to package directions. Cool cupcakes in pans on wire racks 15 minutes; remove from pans and cool completely on wire racks.

3. Beat butter in large bowl with electric mixer until creamy. Gradually add powdered sugar to form very stiff frosting, scraping down side of bowl occasionally. Gradually add half-and-half until frosting is of desired consistency.

4. Generously frost tops of cupcakes.

5. Cut out ear and tongue shapes from fruit roll-ups with scissors; arrange on cupcakes, pressing into frosting as shown in photo. Add candies to create eyes and noses.

Super Cool Cakes

MANDARIN ORANGE TEA CAKE

Makes 16 servings

  1 **package (16 ounces) pound cake mix**
½ **cup plus 2 tablespoons orange juice, divided**
  2 **eggs**
¼ **cup milk**
  1 **can (15 ounces) mandarin orange segments in light syrup, drained**
¾ **cup powdered sugar**
    Grated peel of 1 orange

1. Preheat oven to 350°F. Grease 9-inch bundt pan.

2. Beat cake mix, ½ cup orange juice, eggs and milk in large bowl with electric mixer at medium speed 2 minutes or until light and fluffy. Gently fold in orange segments. Pour batter into prepared pan.

3. Bake 45 minutes or until golden brown and toothpick inserted near center comes out clean. Cool cake in pan on wire rack 15 minutes; invert cake onto wire rack and cool completely.

4. Combine sugar, orange peel and remaining 2 tablespoons orange juice in small bowl; stir until smooth. Drizzle glaze over cake. Allow glaze to set about 5 minutes before serving.

Mandarin Orange Tea Cake

PB & J SANDWICH CAKE

Makes 12 servings

1 package (18¼ ounces) white cake mix with pudding in the mix, plus
   ingredients to prepare mix
¾ cup powdered sugar
5 tablespoons peanut butter
1 tablespoon butter, softened
2 to 3 tablespoons heavy cream or milk
½ cup strawberry or grape jam

1. Preheat oven to 350°F. Grease two 8-inch square baking pans. Prepare cake mix according to package directions. Spread batter in prepared pans.

2. Bake 30 minutes or until toothpick inserted into center comes out clean. Cool in pans on wire racks 30 minutes. Remove from pans and cool completely on wire racks.

3. Carefully slice off browned tops of both cakes to create flat, even layers. Place 1 layer on serving plate, cut side up.

4. Beat powdered sugar, peanut butter, butter and 2 tablespoons cream with electric mixer at medium speed until light and creamy. Add remaining 1 tablespoon cream if necessary to reach spreading consistency. Gently spread filling over cut side of cake layer on serving plate. Spread jam over peanut butter filling. Top with second cake layer, cut side up.

5. Cut cake in half diagonally to resemble sandwich. To serve, cut into thin slices across the diagonal using serrated knife.

POLKA DOT CAKE

Makes 16 servings

1 package (18¼ ounces) chocolate cake mix, plus ingredients to prepare mix

¾ cup white chocolate chips

2 bars (3½ ounces each) good-quality bittersweet or semisweet chocolate, broken into small pieces

¼ cup (½ stick) unsalted butter, cut into small chunks

¼ cup heavy cream

1 tablespoon powdered sugar

Dash salt

¼ cup small chocolate nonpareil candies

1. Preheat oven to 350°F. Generously spray 12-cup bundt pan with nonstick cooking spray.

2. Prepare cake mix according to package directions. Pour batter into prepared pan; sprinkle with chips.

3. Bake 40 minutes or until toothpick inserted near center comes out clean. Cool in pan on wire rack 30 minutes; invert cake onto wire rack and cool completely. Place sheet of waxed paper under wire rack.

4. Combine chocolate, butter, cream, powdered sugar and salt in small, heavy saucepan. Heat over very low heat, stirring constantly, just until butter and chocolate melt. Mixture should be tepid, not hot. Immediately spoon chocolate glaze over cake, spreading to cover side as well as top. Scoop up any glaze from waxed paper and spoon over cake.

5. Arrange nonpareil candies over glaze. Set cake aside about 2 hours or until glaze is set. Do not refrigerate.

PONIES IN THE MEADOW

Makes 9 to 12 servings

1 package (18¼ ounces) cake mix, any flavor, plus ingredients to
   prepare mix
1 cup flaked coconut
   Green food coloring
1 container (16 ounces) white frosting
   Pretzel sticks
2 small plastic ponies

1. Preheat oven to 350°F. Prepare and bake cake mix according to package
directions in two 8-inch square baking pans. Cool in pans on wire racks
10 minutes; remove from pans and cool completely on wire racks.

2. Place coconut in small bowl. Add 4 drops green food coloring; stir until well
blended. Adjust color with additional drops of food coloring, if necessary.

3. Tint frosting with food coloring to desired shade of green. Place 1 cake layer
on serving plate; spread evenly with ½ cup frosting. Top with second cake
layer; frost top and sides of cake with remaining frosting. Scatter coconut
over top of cake.

4. Stand pretzel sticks around edges of cake to create fence; arrange ponies as
desired.

TIP: Additional decorations can be added to the cake, if desired. Arrange candy
rocks or brown jelly beans to create a path. Use the star tip on red or yellow
decorating icing to create flowers in the meadow.

FLAPJACK PARTY STACK

Makes 12 servings

1 package (18¼ ounces) yellow cake mix, plus ingredients to prepare mix
1 container (16 ounces) vanilla frosting
1 quart fresh strawberries, washed, hulled and sliced
1 cup caramel or butterscotch ice cream topping

1. Preheat oven to 350°F. Grease bottoms and sides of four 9-inch round cake pans; line pans with waxed paper.

2. Prepare cake mix according to package directions. Pour batter into prepared pans; bake according to package directions, reducing baking time to compensate for thinner layers.* Cool in pans on wire racks 15 minutes; remove from pans and cool completely on wire racks.

3. Reserve ¼ cup frosting. Place 1 cake layer on serving plate; spread or pipe ⅓ of remaining frosting in swirls on cake to resemble whipped butter. Top with ¼ of sliced strawberries. Repeat with 2 more cake layers, frosting and strawberries. Top stack with remaining cake layer.

4. Heat caramel topping in microwave just until pourable. Drizzle over top of cake. Spread or pipe remaining frosting in center; garnish with remaining strawberries.

*If you don't have four 9-inch round cake pans, prepare two 9-inch pans as directed in Step 1. Divide batter evenly between pans and bake according to package directions. Cut each layer horizontally in half when cool.

BUTTERSCOTCH BUNDT CAKE

Makes 12 to 16 servings

1 package (18¼ ounces) yellow cake mix *without* pudding in the mix
1 package (4-serving size) butterscotch-flavor instant pudding and
    pie filling mix
1 cup water
3 eggs
2 teaspoons ground cinnamon
½ cup chopped pecans
    Powdered sugar (optional)

1. Preheat oven to 325°F. Spray 12-cup bundt pan with nonstick cooking spray.

2. Beat cake mix, pudding mix, water, eggs and cinnamon in large bowl with electric mixer at medium-high speed 2 minutes or until blended. Stir in pecans. Pour into prepared pan.

3. Bake 40 to 50 minutes or until cake springs back when lightly touched. Cool in pan on wire rack 10 minutes; invert cake onto serving plate and cool completely. Sprinkle with powdered sugar, if desired.

PISTACHIO WALNUT BUNDT CAKE: Substitute white cake mix for yellow cake mix, pistachio-flavored pudding for butterscotch pudding and walnuts for pecans.

To dust a cake with powdered sugar, place the sugar in a small strainer and gently shake the strainer over the cake. (Make sure the cake is completely cool first.)

COOKIE PIZZA CAKE

Makes 12 to 14 servings

1 package (18 ounces) refrigerated chocolate chip cookie dough
1 package (18¼ ounces) chocolate cake mix, plus ingredients to
    prepare mix
1 cup prepared vanilla frosting
½ cup peanut butter
1 to 2 tablespoons milk
1 container (16 ounces) chocolate frosting
    Chocolate peanut butter cups, chopped (optional)

1. Preheat oven to 350°F. Spray two 12×1-inch round pizza pans with nonstick cooking spray. Press cookie dough evenly into one pan. Bake 15 to 20 minutes or until edges are golden brown. Cool in pan on wire rack 20 minutes. Remove from pan and cool completely on wire rack.

2. Prepare cake mix according to package directions. Fill second pan ¼ to ½ full with batter. (Reserve remaining cake batter for another use, such as cupcakes.) Bake 10 to 15 minutes or until toothpick inserted into center comes out clean. Cool in pan on wire rack 15 minutes. Gently remove cake from pan and cool completely on wire rack.

3. Blend vanilla frosting and peanut butter in small bowl. Gradually stir in milk, 1 tablespoon at a time, until mixture is of spreadable consistency.

4. Place cookie on serving plate. Spread peanut butter frosting over cookie. Place cake on top of frosting, trimming cookie edge to match cake edge, if necessary. Frost top and side of cake with chocolate frosting. Garnish with peanut butter cups, if desired.

BUCKET OF SAND CAKE

Makes 10 to 12 servings

   1 package (18¼ ounces) banana or butter pecan cake mix, plus
     ingredients to prepare mix
½ teaspoon ground cinnamon
¼ teaspoon ground nutmeg
   1 package (6-serving size) butterscotch-flavor instant pudding and pie
     filling mix, plus ingredients to prepare mix
    Clean plastic beach pail and shovel
1½ cups graham cracker or shortbread cookie crumbs, divided
    Gummy fish and octopus, starfish and seashell candies, green string
     candy and mini chocolate chips

1. Preheat oven to 350°F. Prepare and bake cake mix according to package directions in two 9-inch round cake pans, stirring cinnamon and nutmeg into batter. Cool in pans on wire racks 10 minutes; remove from pans and cool completely on wire racks.

2. Meanwhile, prepare pudding mix according to package directions.

3. Cut 1 cake layer into 1-inch slices; arrange about ⅓ of slices in bottom of pail. Spoon ⅓ of pudding over cake slices; top with ⅓ of cake slices. Repeat layers with ⅓ of pudding and remaining cake slices. Sprinkle with 1 cup graham cracker crumbs. Place shovel in cake and decorate with gummy fish and other candies as desired.

4. Cut second cake layer in half horizontally. Place one half, cut side up, on serving tray or plate. Place pail on top of cake layer as shown in photo. Break remaining cake layer into chunks; arrange around base of pail. Spoon remaining pudding over cake chunks; sprinkle remaining ½ cup graham cracker crumbs over pudding. Decorate with candies as desired. To serve, use shovel to spoon cake onto plates.

PEPPERMINT MOUNTAIN RANGE

Makes 16 servings

1 package (18¼ ounces) white or yellow cake mix *without* pudding in
   the mix
1 package (4-serving size) vanilla instant pudding and pie filling mix
1 cup sour cream
4 eggs
½ cup vegetable oil
⅓ cup water
¾ teaspoon peppermint extract
   Red food coloring
1 cup mini chocolate chips
2 cups sifted powdered sugar
2 to 3 tablespoons milk
½ cup crushed peppermint candies (about 12 round candies)

1. Preheat oven to 350°F. Grease and flour 12-cup bundt pan.

2. Beat cake mix, pudding mix, sour cream, eggs, oil and water in large bowl
with electric mixer at low speed about 1 minute or until blended. Increase
speed to medium; beat 1 to 2 minutes or until smooth.

3. Combine 1½ cups batter, peppermint extract and 16 drops red food coloring
in small bowl; mix well. Stir chocolate chips into remaining batter. Spread half
of chocolate chip batter in prepared pan. Spoon peppermint batter on top. Spread
remaining chocolate chip batter over peppermint batter.

4. Bake 50 to 60 minutes or until toothpick inserted near center comes out
clean. Cool in pan on wire rack 20 minutes; invert cake onto wire rack and
cool completely.

5. Blend powdered sugar and 2 tablespoons milk in small bowl until smooth.
Add remaining 1 tablespoon milk if necessary to reach drizzling consistency.
Drizzle glaze over cooled cake. Sprinkle with crushed candies.

LEMON-ORANGE PARTY CAKE

Makes 20 servings

1 package (18¼ ounces) yellow cake mix with pudding in the mix
1¼ cups plus 5 tablespoons orange juice, divided
3 eggs
⅓ cup vegetable oil
2 tablespoons grated orange peel
5½ cups sifted powdered sugar, divided
⅓ cup lemon juice
⅓ cup butter, softened
Multi-colored sprinkles
20 jellied orange or lemon slices

1. Preheat oven to 350°F. Lightly grease 13×9-inch baking pan.

2. Beat cake mix, 1¼ cups orange juice, eggs, oil and orange peel in large bowl with electric mixer at low speed about 1 minute or until blended. Increase speed to medium; beat 1 to 2 minutes or until smooth. Spread in prepared pan.

3. Bake 33 to 38 minutes or until toothpick inserted into center comes out clean. Meanwhile, combine 1 cup powdered sugar and lemon juice in small bowl; stir until smooth.

4. Pierce top of warm cake generously with large fork or wooden skewer (about ½-inch intervals). Slowly drizzle lemon glaze over warm cake. Cool completely.

5. Beat remaining 4½ cups powdered sugar and butter in large bowl with electric mixer at low speed until combined. Beat in enough remaining orange juice to reach spreading consistency. Gently spread frosting over cooled cake. Decorate top of cake with sprinkles and jellied fruit slices.

CANDY BAR CAKE

Makes 12 servings

1 package (18¼ ounces) devil's food cake mix *without* pudding in the mix

1 cup sour cream

4 eggs

⅓ cup vegetable oil

¼ cup water

3 containers (16 ounces each) white frosting

1 bar (2.1 ounces) chocolate-covered crispy peanut butter candy, chopped

1 bar (2.07 ounces) chocolate-covered peanut, caramel and nougat candy, chopped

1 bar (1.4 ounces) chocolate-covered toffee candy, chopped

4 bars (1.55 ounces each) milk chocolate

1. Preheat oven to 350°F. Grease and flour two 9-inch round cake pans.

2. Beat cake mix, sour cream, eggs, oil and water in large bowl with electric mixer at low speed about 1 minute or until blended. Increase speed to medium; beat 1 to 2 minutes or until smooth. Spread batter in prepared pans.

3. Bake 30 to 35 minutes or until toothpick inserted into center comes out clean. Cool in pans on wire racks 10 minutes. Remove from pans and cool completely on wire racks.

4. Cut each cake layer in half horizontally. Place 1 cake layer on serving plate. Spread generously with frosting. Sprinkle with 1 chopped candy bar. Repeat with 2 more cake layers, additional frosting and remaining 2 chopped candy bars. Top with remaining cake layer; frost top of cake with remaining frosting.

5. Break milk chocolate bars into pieces along score lines. Stand chocolate pieces in frosting around outside edge of cake as shown in photo.

COOKIES 'N' CREAM CAKE

Makes 10 to 12 servings

1 package (18¼ ounces) white cake mix *without* pudding in the mix
1 package (4-serving size) white chocolate-flavor instant pudding and
    pie filling mix
1 cup vegetable oil
4 egg whites
½ cup milk
20 chocolate sandwich cookies, coarsely chopped
½ cup semisweet chocolate chips
1 teaspoon shortening
4 chocolate sandwich cookies, cut into quarters for garnish

1. Preheat oven to 350°F. Spray 12-cup bundt pan with nonstick cooking spray.

2. Beat cake mix, pudding mix, oil, egg whites and milk in large bowl with electric mixer at medium speed 2 minutes or until ingredients are well blended. Stir in chopped cookies; spread batter in prepared pan.

3. Bake 50 to 60 minutes or until cake springs back when lightly touched. Cool 1 hour in pan on wire rack; invert cake onto serving plate and cool completely.

4. Combine chocolate chips and shortening in small microwavable bowl. Microwave at HIGH 30 seconds; stir. Microwave at 15-second intervals as necessary, stirring until melted and smooth. Drizzle glaze over cake and garnish with quartered cookies.

HIDDEN SURPRISE CAKE

Makes 12 servings

1 package (16 ounces) angel food cake mix, plus ingredients to
   prepare mix
1 ½ to 2 pints chocolate ice cream, softened
2 cups heavy cream, well chilled
½ cup unsweetened cocoa powder
6 tablespoons powdered sugar
2 to 4 tablespoons mini chocolate chips (optional)

1. Prepare, bake and cool angel food cake according to package directions.

2. Place cake on work surface. Using serrated knife, cut horizontally across
cake about 1 inch from top. Remove top of cake; set aside.

3. Scoop out inside of cake with hands, leaving 1 inch shell on side and
bottom. (Be careful not to tear through cake.) Spoon ice cream into cake,
packing down. Cover with cake top.

4. Beat cream and cocoa in large bowl with electric mixer at medium speed
until slightly thickened. Gradually beat in powdered sugar at high speed until
stiff peaks form. Cover top and side of cake with chocolate whipped cream.
Sprinkle with chocolate chips, if desired. Serve immediately.

NOTE: The cake can be baked and filled up to one week in advance. Wrap well
in heavy-duty aluminum foil and store in the freezer. Remove 15 minutes before
frosting. Serve immediately after frosting.

Great Girl Cakes

RAINBOW CAKE

Makes 5 cakes

1 (18¼ ounces) cake mix, any flavor, plus ingredients to prepare mix
⅓ cup seedless raspberry jam
1 container (16 ounces) vanilla frosting
  Multi-colored coated fruit candies

1. Preheat oven to 350°F. Prepare and bake cake mix according to package directions in 17×11-inch jelly-roll pan. Cool completely in pan on wire rack.

2. Using knife or square cookie cutter, cut 15 (2½-inch) squares from cake. Spread raspberry jam on 1 layer. Top with second cake layer and spread with jam. Top with third cake layer.

3. Frost entire cake with vanilla frosting. Repeat to make 5 cakes. Sprinkle with candies or decorate as desired.

Rainbow Cake

INDIVIDUAL FLOWER POT CAKES

Makes 18 cakes

18 (4×2½-inch) sterilized unglazed terra cotta flower pots*
1 package (18¼ ounces) dark chocolate cake mix, plus ingredients to
    prepare mix
1 package (12 ounces) semisweet chocolate chips
1 container (16 ounces) chocolate frosting
8 to 10 chocolate sandwich cookies, broken
   Plastic drinking straws
   Assorted candies such as lollipops, spearmint leaf jelly candies and
      gummy worms
   Decorating icing (optional)

Wash and dry pots. Place in 350°F oven 3 hours to sterilize. Remove from oven; cool completely.

1. Preheat oven to 350°F. Grease flower pots generously; line bottoms with greased parchment paper.

2. Prepare cake mix according to package directions; stir chocolate chips into batter.

3. Place pots in standard (2½-inch) muffin pan cups; spoon batter into pots, filling ½ full. Bake for 35 to 40 minutes or until toothpick inserted into centers comes out clean. Remove pots from muffin pans; cool completely on wire racks.

4. Place cookies in food processor; process using on/off pulses until coarse crumbs form.

5. Frost tops of cakes with chocolate frosting. Sprinkle cookie crumbs over frosting to resemble dirt. Decorate with lollipop flowers**, spearmint leaves and gummy worms.

**Lollipop Flowers: Push straws into each flower pot for "stems." Use scissors to trim straws to different heights. Insert lollipops into straw stems. Pipe decorating icing onto lollipops to create petals and centers of flowers, if desired.*

SLEEPOVER CAKE

Makes 12 servings

1 package (18¼ ounces) cake mix, any flavor, plus ingredients to
    prepare mix
1 container (16 ounces) white frosting
    Red food coloring
2 long cream-filled snack cakes
    Decorative sugar sprinkles
4 marshmallows
    Red and yellow decorating icing
4 chocolate peanut butter cups (milk or white chocolate)
    Red, black or brown licorice strips (optional)
2 packages (6 feet each) bubble gum tape (pink and green)
    Bear-shaped graham crackers

1. Preheat oven to 350°F. Prepare and bake cake mix according to package
directions in 13×9-inch pan. Cool in pan on wire rack 10 minutes; remove
from pan and cool completely on wire rack.

2. Tint frosting with food coloring to desired shade of pink. Place cake on
serving platter; frost top and sides with pink frosting.

3. Cut snack cakes in half lengthwise. Arrange snack cakes, cut sides down,
evenly on top of frosted cake. Smooth frosting over snack cakes; sprinkle
with decorative sugar sprinkles.

4. Flatten marshmallows by pressing down firmly with palm of hand. Arrange
marshmallows at top of snack cakes to create pillows. Use decorating icing to
create eyes and lips on peanut butter cups. Add licorice strips for hair, if desired.
Place decorated peanut butter cups on marshmallow pillows.

5. Unwind bubble gum tape; arrange across cake at edge of peanut butter cups
to form edge of blanket. Arrange second bubble gum tape around base of cake.
Tuck bear-shaped graham crackers around blanket.

Great Girl Cakes

BIG PURPLE PURSE

Makes 8 to 10 servings

1 package (18¼ ounces) cake mix, any flavor, plus ingredients to
    prepare mix
1 container (16 ounces) white frosting
   Red and blue food coloring
1 piece red licorice rope
1 white chocolate-coated pretzel
   Round sugar-coated colored candies
   Candy lipstick, necklace and ring (optional)

1. Preheat oven to 350°F. Prepare and bake cake mix according to package directions in two 9-inch round cake pans. Cool in pans on wire racks 10 minutes; remove from pans and cool completely on wire racks. Reserve 1 cake layer for another use.

2. Add 4 drops of each food coloring to frosting; mix well. Add additional food coloring, one drop at a time, to reach desired shade of purple.

3. Spread about ½ cup frosting over top of cake layer. Cut cake in half; press frosted sides together to form half circle. Place cake, flat side down, on serving plate.

4. Spread frosting over top and sides of cake. Cut licorice rope in half; press ends into top of cake to form purse handle. Add pretzel for clasp. Gently press round candies into sides of cake. Arrange candy lipstick, necklace and ring around cake, if desired.

BEAUTIFUL BUTTERFLIES

Makes 6 butterflies (2 servings each)

1 package (18¼ ounces) yellow cake mix with pudding in the mix, plus
    ingredients to prepare mix
6 cups powdered sugar
¾ cup unsalted butter, at room temperature
¾ cup milk or half-and-half
¼ teaspoon salt
    Blue and green food coloring
    Colored candies and mini candy-coated chocolate pieces
    Red licorice string, cut into 1-inch pieces

1. Preheat oven to 350°F. Prepare and bake cake mix according to package directions in 12-cup bundt pan. Cool in pan on wire rack 15 minutes; invert onto wire rack and cool completely.

2. Beat powdered sugar, butter, milk and salt in large bowl with electric mixer until light and creamy. Divide frosting between 2 bowls. Tint 1 bowl blue and 1 bowl green (or use only one color, if desired).

3. Cut cake into 4 quarters; cut each quarter into 6 slices to create 24 slices. Cut thin strip from inside of 12 cake slices.

4. For each butterfly, arrange 2 cake strips vertically in center of plate for body. Spread with tinted frosting. Place 1 trimmed cake slice on each side of body. Place 1 larger cake slice on each side of body next to small slices as shown in photo. Repeat with remaining cake strips and slices.

5. Decorate with tinted frosting and candies as desired. Arrange 2 pieces licorice at top of each butterfly body for antennae.

FLOWER POWER STRAWBERRY CAKE

Makes 15 servings

1 package (18¼ ounces) white cake mix *without* pudding in the mix
2 containers (6 ounces each) strawberry-flavor yogurt
4 eggs
⅓ cup vegetable oil
1 package (4-serving size) strawberry-flavor gelatin
1 container (8 ounces) frozen whipped dessert topping, thawed
12 to 13 medium strawberries
   Yellow food coloring

1. Preheat oven to 350°F. Lightly grease 13×9-inch baking pan.

2. Beat cake mix, yogurt, eggs, oil and gelatin in large bowl with electric mixer at low speed about 1 minute or until blended. Increase speed to medium; beat 1 to 2 minutes or until smooth. Spread batter in prepared pan.

3. Bake 38 to 43 minutes or until toothpick inserted into center comes out clean. Cool completely in pan on wire rack.

4. Reserve ½ cup whipped topping. Spread remaining topping over cooled cake. Cut each strawberry lengthwise into 6 wedges. Use strawberry wedges to create 15 flowers on top of cake. For each flower, arrange 5 strawberry wedges, pointed end towards center, to create flower petals as shown in photo.

5. Tint reserved whipped topping with 6 to 8 drops yellow food coloring. Place tinted topping in plastic food storage bag; cut off ⅛ inch from corner of bag. Pipe yellow topping into center of each flower. Serve cake immediately or loosely cover and refrigerate up to 24 hours.

PRETTY PACKAGE CAKE

Makes 12 to 16 servings

CAKE

    1 package (18¼ ounces) lemon cake mix, plus ingredients to prepare mix
    1 container (16 ounces) lemon frosting

RIBBON

    2 cups powdered sugar, sifted
    1 cup marshmallow creme
    Red food coloring

COOKIE GARNISH (OPTIONAL)

    1 package (18 ounces) refrigerated sugar cookie dough
    Decorating icing

1. Prepare and bake cake mix according to package directions in two 8-inch square baking pans. Cool completely in pans on wire racks.

2. Remove cake layers from pans. Fill and frost cake with lemon frosting.

3. For ribbon, combine powdered sugar and marshmallow creme in medium bowl; stir until blended. Knead by hand until mixture comes together into stiff, workable dough. (Sprinkle sifted powdered sugar on hands often to keep dough from sticking.) Knead in 2 or 3 drops food coloring until desired color is reached.

4. Roll dough with rolling pin to ¼-inch thickness, sprinkling with sifted powdered sugar if necessary to keep dough from sticking. Cut dough into 1½-inch-wide strips. Place strips over frosted cake to form ribbon and bow as shown in photo; trim ends.

5. For cookie garnish, prepare and bake 2-inch round cookies according to package directions. Cool on wire rack. Pipe flowers onto cooled cookies with decorating icing. Garnish cake with cookies, if desired.

TIP: This great all-occasion cake can be easily customized for any celebration. Simply frost with appropriate colors and decorate the cookies to match the theme.

Halloween Treats

BLUE GOO CUPCAKES

Makes 24 cupcakes

1 package (18¼ ounces) white cake mix, plus ingredients to prepare mix
  Blue food coloring
1 package (6 ounces) blue gelatin
1⅓ cups boiling water
  Blue decorating icing

1. Preheat oven to 350°F. Line 24 standard (2½-inch) muffin pan cups with paper liners.

2. Prepare cake mix according to package directions. Add 6 drops blue food coloring to batter; adjust color as desired. Spoon batter into prepared muffin cups, filling ⅔ full. Bake according to package directions. Cool cupcakes in pans on wire racks 5 minutes; remove from pans and cool completely on wire racks.

3. Meanwhile, combine gelatin and boiling water in small bowl. Stir mixture 3 minutes or until gelatin is completely dissolved. Freeze mixture 40 minutes, stirring often, or until partially set.

4. Pipe ring of blue icing around edge of each cupcake. Spoon 1 rounded tablespoon gelatin mixture onto each cupcake.

TIP: For a firm texture, chill cupcakes. For a runny consistency, serve at room temperature.

Blue Goo Cupcakes

BOO HANDS CUPCAKES

Makes 24 cupcakes

1 package (18¼ ounces) chocolate cake mix, plus ingredients to
    prepare mix
1 container (16 ounces) white frosting
36 marshmallows
24 black jelly beans, cut into halves
12 orange jelly beans, cut into halves

1. Preheat oven to 350°F. Line 24 standard (2½-inch) muffin pan cups with paper liners or spray with nonstick cooking spray.

2. Prepare cake mix and bake in prepared muffin cups according to package directions. Cool cupcakes in pans on wire racks 15 minutes; remove from pans and cool completely on wire racks.

3. Spread small amount of frosting on cupcake. Cut 1 marshmallow in half crosswise and place on cupcake. Frost again, completely covering marshmallow half.

4. Roll marshmallow between your hands until it is about 2½ inches long. Cut in half and arrange halves on either side of cupcake to create hands; cover completely with frosting.

5. Decorate ghost face using 2 black jelly bean halves for eyes and orange jelly bean half for nose. Swirl frosting on top of ghost as shown in photo. Repeat with remaining cupcakes.

WOLFMAN CAKE

Makes 12 servings

1 package (18¼ ounces) cake mix, any flavor, plus ingredients to
  prepare mix
1 container (16 ounces) chocolate frosting
1 container (16 ounces) caramel frosting
  Hard candy or nuts, large candy corn, yellow gummy worms and
    black jelly beans
  Black and red decorating gels

1. Preheat oven to 350°F. Prepare and bake cake mix according to package
directions in 13×9-inch baking pan. Cool cake in pan on wire rack 15 minutes;
remove cake from pan and cool completely on wire rack.

2. Cut cake in half crosswise to form two 6½×4½-inch layers. Place 1 layer
on serving platter. Spread ½ of chocolate frosting over bottom layer. Top with
second layer. Spread remaining chocolate frosting over top and sides of cake.

3. Spoon caramel frosting over top of cake. Use back of spoon to pull frosting
into points to resemble fur. Decorate face with assorted candies and decorating
gels as desired.

*Before frosting a cake,
brush all the crumbs from the
surfaces. Freezing the cake
for 20 minutes will also
make it easier to frost.*

Wolfman Cake

OOZE CUPCAKES

Makes 24 cupcakes

1 package (8 ounces) cream cheese, softened
½ cup powdered sugar
⅓ cup thawed frozen limeade concentrate
1 teaspoon vanilla
   Yellow and green food coloring
1 package (18¼ ounces) chocolate cake mix, plus ingredients to
   prepare mix
1 container (16 ounces) vanilla frosting
   Orange sugar

1. Preheat oven to 350°F. Line 24 standard (2½-inch) muffin pan cups with paper liners or spray with nonstick cooking spray.

2. Combine cream cheese, powdered sugar, limeade concentrate and vanilla in large bowl. Beat with electric mixer at medium speed until well blended. Tint with yellow food coloring; beat until well blended.

3. Prepare cake mix according to package directions using 1 egg instead of number of eggs directions call for, water and vegetable oil as directed on package. Spoon batter into prepared muffin cups, filling half full. Spoon 1 rounded teaspoon cream cheese mixture into center of each cup.

4. Bake about 20 minutes or until toothpick inserted into centers comes out clean. Cool cupcakes in pans on wire racks 10 minutes; remove from pans and cool completely on wire racks.

5. Tint frosting with green food coloring to desired shade of green; stir until well blended. Spread frosting on cooled cupcakes. Sprinkle with orange sugar.

LITTLE DEVILS

Makes 18 cupcakes

1 package (18¼ ounces) carrot cake mix
3 eggs
½ cup solid-pack pumpkin
⅓ cup vegetable oil
1 container (16 ounces) cream cheese frosting
Assorted Halloween candies, jelly beans, chocolate candies and nuts

1. Preheat oven to 350°F. Line 18 standard (2½-inch) muffin pan cups with paper liners.

2. Prepare cake mix according to package directions, using water as directed on package, eggs, pumpkin and oil. Spoon batter into prepared muffin cups.

3. Bake 20 minutes or until toothpick inserted into centers comes out clean. Cool cupcakes in pans on wire racks 5 minutes; remove from pans and cool completely on wire racks.

4. Frost cupcakes with cream cheese frosting. Decorate cupcakes with assorted candies.

Store canned pumpkin in a cool, dry place for up to one year. Refrigerate any leftover pumpkin in a tightly covered nonmetal container for up to five days.

PUMPKIN BUNDTINGS WITH CIDER GLAZE

Makes 12 servings

CAKES

1 package (18¼ ounces) spice cake mix
1 can (16 ounces) solid-pack pumpkin
1⅓ cups water
3 eggs
⅓ cup vegetable oil
1 teaspoon vanilla

GLAZE

4 cups plus 2 tablespoons apple cider, divided
16 whole cloves
4 cinnamon sticks or 2 teaspoons ground cinnamon
1½ teaspoons cornstarch
¾ cup caramel ice cream topping (optional)

1. Preheat oven to 350°F. Grease and flour 12 (½-cup) mini bundt pans.

2. For cakes, combine all cake ingredients in large bowl; mix well. Spoon batter evenly into prepared pans. Bake 30 minutes or until toothpick inserted near centers comes out clean. Cool cakes in pans on wire racks 15 minutes; remove from pans and cool completely on wire racks.

3. For glaze, combine 4 cups apple cider, cloves and cinnamon sticks in nonstick skillet; bring to a boil over high heat. Boil 7 minutes or until liquid has reduced to 1 cup. Meanwhile, combine remaining 2 tablespoons apple cider and cornstarch in small bowl; stir until cornstarch is dissolved.

4. When cider mixture is reduced, add cornstarch mixture to skillet. Cook and stir until slightly thickened. Remove from heat; cool completely.

5. Remove cloves and cinnamon sticks from glaze; discard. Spoon about 1 tablespoon glaze over each cake. Drizzle 1 tablespoon caramel topping around outer edge of each cake, if desired.

SPIDER CUPCAKES

Makes 24 to 27 cupcakes

    1 package (18¼ ounces) yellow or white cake mix
    1 cup solid-pack pumpkin
    ¾ cup water
    3 eggs
    2 tablespoons vegetable oil
    1 teaspoon ground cinnamon
    1 teaspoon pumpkin pie spice
    1 container (16 ounces) vanilla, cream cheese or caramel frosting
       Orange food coloring
    4 ounces semisweet chocolate
  48 black gumdrops

1. Preheat oven to 350°F. Line 24 standard (2½-inch) muffin pan cups with paper liners or spray with nonstick cooking spray.

2. Beat cake mix, pumpkin, water, eggs, oil, cinnamon and pumpkin pie spice in large bowl with electric mixer at medium speed 3 minutes or until well blended.

3. Spoon ¼ cup batter into each muffin cup. Bake about 20 minutes or until toothpick inserted into centers comes out clean. Cool cupcakes in pans on wire racks 10 minutes; remove from pans and cool completely on wire racks.

4. Tint frosting with food coloring. Adjust to desired shade of orange by adding additional food coloring, 1 drop at a time; stir until well blended. Frost cupcakes.

5. Place chocolate in small resealable plastic food storage bag. Microwave at MEDIUM (50% power) 40 seconds. Knead bag; microwave 30 seconds to 1 minute or until chocolate is melted. Knead bag until chocolate is smooth. Cut off small corner of bag; drizzle chocolate in 4 or 5 concentric circles on top of cupcake. Immediately draw 6 to 8 lines from center to edge of cupcake with toothpick or knife to create web. Repeat with remaining cupcakes and chocolate.

6. For spider, place 1 gumdrop in center of web on top of cupcake. Flatten another gumdrop with rolling pin on generously sugared surface. Cut into 6 thin slices; roll slices between hands to create legs. Arrange legs around gumdrop to complete spider. Repeat with remaining gumdrops and cupcakes.

SCAREDY CAT CAKE

Makes 12 servings

1 package (18¼ ounces) devil's food cake mix, plus ingredients to
    prepare mix
1 container (16 ounces) dark chocolate fudge frosting
4 individual square chocolate snack cakes
1 large orange or pink gumdrop
    Granulated sugar
    Black decorating gel
    Black string licorice, cut into 3½- to 4-inch lengths
2 large yellow gumdrops

1. Prepare and bake cake mix according to package directions in two 8-inch round baking pans. Cool cake layers in pans on wire racks 15 minutes; remove from pans and cool completely on wire racks.

2. Place one layer upside down on serving platter; spread with chocolate frosting. Top with second cake layer, top side up. Frost top and side of cake.

3. Cut snack cakes in half diagonally. Frost tops of all snack cake triangles. Make 2 stacks of 4 triangles each. Place at top of round cake to create ears; frost to blend in with round cake. Use back of spoon to pull frosting on side of cake into points to resemble fur.

4. Flatten orange gumdrop with rolling pin on generously sugared surface. Cut out large triangle; place in center of cake for nose. Use decorating gel to create mouth and licorice for whiskers.

5. Flatten yellow gumdrops with rolling pin on generously sugared surface. Cut out pointed oval shapes; place on cake for eyes. Pipe gel onto eyes.

MAGICAL WIZARD HATS

Makes 24 cupcakes

1 package (18¼ ounces) cake mix, any flavor, plus ingredients to
    prepare mix
2 containers (16 ounces each) vanilla frosting
    Yellow and purple or black food coloring
2 packages (4 ounces each) sugar cones
    Orange sugar, decors and black decorating gel

1. Line 24 standard (2½-inch) muffin pan cups with paper liners or spray with nonstick cooking spray.

2. Prepare cake mix and bake in prepared muffin cups according to package directions. Cool cupcakes in pans on wire racks 15 minutes; remove from pans and cool completely on wire racks.

3. Frost cupcakes. Place ½ cup remaining frosting in small bowl; tint with yellow food coloring. Tint remaining frosting with purple or black food coloring.

4. Spread sugar cones with dark frosting, covering completely. Place 1 cone upside down on each frosted cupcake. Spoon yellow frosting into small resealable plastic food storage bag. Cut off small corner of bag; pipe yellow frosting around base of each frosted cone. Decorate as desired with orange sugar, decors and black decorating gel.

Index

METRIC CONVERSION CHART

VOLUME MEASUREMENTS (dry)

$1/8$ teaspoon = 0.5 mL
$1/4$ teaspoon = 1 mL
$1/2$ teaspoon = 2 mL
$3/4$ teaspoon = 4 mL
1 teaspoon = 5 mL
1 tablespoon = 15 mL
2 tablespoons = 30 mL
$1/4$ cup = 60 mL
$1/3$ cup = 75 mL
$1/2$ cup = 125 mL
$2/3$ cup = 150 mL
$3/4$ cup = 175 mL
1 cup = 250 mL
2 cups = 1 pint = 500 mL
3 cups = 750 mL
4 cups = 1 quart = 1 L

VOLUME MEASUREMENTS (fluid)

1 fluid ounce (2 tablespoons) = 30 mL
4 fluid ounces ($1/2$ cup) = 125 mL
8 fluid ounces (1 cup) = 250 mL
12 fluid ounces ($1 1/2$ cups) = 375 mL
16 fluid ounces (2 cups) = 500 mL

WEIGHTS (mass)

$1/2$ ounce = 15 g
1 ounce = 30 g
3 ounces = 90 g
4 ounces = 120 g
8 ounces = 225 g
10 ounces = 285 g
12 ounces = 360 g
16 ounces = 1 pound = 450 g

DIMENSIONS

$1/16$ inch = 2 mm
$1/8$ inch = 3 mm
$1/4$ inch = 6 mm
$1/2$ inch = 1.5 cm
$3/4$ inch = 2 cm
1 inch = 2.5 cm

OVEN TEMPERATURES

250°F = 120°C
275°F = 140°C
300°F = 150°C
325°F = 160°C
350°F = 180°C
375°F = 190°C
400°F = 200°C
425°F = 220°C
450°F = 230°C

BAKING PAN SIZES

Utensil	Size in Inches/Quarts	Metric Volume	Size in Centimeters
Baking or Cake Pan (square or rectangular)	$8 \times 8 \times 2$	2 L	$20 \times 20 \times 5$
	$9 \times 9 \times 2$	2.5 L	$23 \times 23 \times 5$
	$12 \times 8 \times 2$	3 L	$30 \times 20 \times 5$
	$13 \times 9 \times 2$	3.5 L	$33 \times 23 \times 5$
Loaf Pan	$8 \times 4 \times 3$	1.5 L	$20 \times 10 \times 7$
	$9 \times 5 \times 3$	2 L	$23 \times 13 \times 7$
Round Layer Cake Pan	$8 \times 1 1/2$	1.2 L	20×4
	$9 \times 1 1/2$	1.5 L	23×4
Pie Plate	$8 \times 1 1/4$	750 mL	20×3
	$9 \times 1 1/4$	1 L	23×3
Baking Dish or Casserole	1 quart	1 L	—
	$1 1/2$ quart	1.5 L	—
	2 quart	2 L	—

Homecoming: Special Foods, Special Memories
Baylor University Alumni Association
P.O. Box 97116
Waco, TX 76798-7116

Please send _____ copies of *Homecoming* @ $16.95 each _____
Postage and handling @ $ 2.00 each _____
Texas residents add sales tax @ $ 1.40 each _____
TOTAL _____

Name _____

Address _____

City _____ State _____ Zip _____

Make checks payable to B.A.S.E.

Homecoming: Special Foods, Special Memories
Baylor University Alumni Association
P.O. Box 97116
Waco, TX 76798-7116

Please send _____ copies of *Homecoming* @ $16.95 each _____
Postage and handling @ $ 2.00 each _____
Texas residents add sales tax @ $ 1.40 each _____
TOTAL _____

Name _____

Address _____

City _____ State _____ Zip _____

Make checks payable to B.A.S.E.

Homecoming: Special Foods, Special Memories
Baylor University Alumni Association
P.O. Box 97116
Waco, TX 76798-7116

Please send _____ copies of *Homecoming* @ $16.95 each _____
Postage and handling @ $ 2.00 each _____
Texas residents add sales tax @ $ 1.40 each _____
TOTAL _____

Name _____

Address _____

City _____ State _____ Zip _____

Make checks payable to B.A.S.E.